LIVING THE CORE VALUES

Self-coaching questions,
inspiration, tips, and
practical exercises for
becoming an awesome
manager

⌘

Managerial Competencies Series
Playbook No. 1

CÉLESTE GRIMARD

CreateSpace, Charleston, SC USA

⌘

ACKNOWLEDGMENTS

I originally developed this series as a self-study, self-paced program for hundreds of managers working in a geographically dispersed area. Over the span of many years, these awesome managers offered me feedback, inspiration, and encouragement to transform this program into a series of practical, easy to read books accessible to all managers. Thank you! I also thank Rhiannon Ward for her assistance in editing and proofreading the books in this series.

CONTENTS

Welcome to the Managerial Competencies Series!

The aim of this series is to help you understand and build the core competencies you need to become an awesome manager.

There's no getting around it. There are tons of journals, books, blogs, videos – you name it – on the topic of managing. Yes, a lot has been written and said about how to be an effective manager. Everyone has their own spin to put on this topic, and research studies on this topic are practically endless. How does a busy manager sort through all the fads and fashions to find the nuggets of wisdom?

In designing this series, I pored over loads of resources and talked with hundreds of managers. I set aside all the fashions, fads, and fantasies, and I extracted only what is likely to be of enduring value to you. Although this series is geared towards practical, immediate use, I hope that it will provoke you to think deeply about managing and your role as a manager, and that it will make a difference for you so you can make a difference for others.

This module – Living the Core Values – is the first of 15 books, each covering one key competency of awesome managers. **Turn to page 79 to learn more about this series**, including the full slate of books, how each book is structured, and tips on how to get the most out of them.

Throughout the book, I will refer to your **learning journal** and your **feedback team. These helpful tools are explained on pages 94 and 95.**

LIVING THE CORE VALUES: INTRODUCTION

Competent managers exemplify core managerial values by demonstrating honesty, truthfulness, trustworthiness, reliability, fairness, and ethicality.

LIVING THE CORE VALUES

Know thyself.

This inscription over the Oracle at Delphi may seem simple enough, but it's probably one of the most challenging tasks that you will undertake. To know yourself is to come face to face with your strengths and weaknesses and, in a sense, to acknowledge your humanity. The process of self-examination is necessary for self-understanding that, in turn, fuels your personal growth and effectiveness. Given that personal effectiveness is the foundation of interpersonal effectiveness, and interpersonal effectiveness is a requirement for leadership, developing yourself as a leader is impossible without it. In other words, before you can effectively lead others, you must be able to lead yourself. As argued by leadership researcher Peter Block, "you cannot give to others what you have not claimed for yourself."

The most direct route to knowing yourself is to consider what you value. Unlike aspects of personality that may change from situation to situation, values serve as the enduring foundation for who we are as human beings. Your values are an indicator of your character. Because they serve as a lens through which you view the world, your values color and shape your thoughts, emotions, and behaviors in any given situation. For example, if you value justice, then you are especially sensitive to any *justices* and injustices that are dealt to you and others.

Think about the last time that you felt strongly about a decision that was made in your workplace. It's likely that your values were being summoned and perhaps even challenged. Values guide and motivate our actions; we are usually willing to direct intense and persistent effort toward something that is consistent with our values. It's important, then, to use them as your lens for understanding yourself. By understanding and developing your values, you find the drive to take action. And every action that you take is a signal of how you expect your clients and staff to be treated, and how you expect to be treated yourself.

LIVING THE CORE VALUES

There are literally hundreds of values that people may possess. In this book, we consider six interlocked values that are at the heart of awesome managers. They represent the foundations of integrity: honesty, truthfulness, trustworthiness, reliability, fairness, and ethicality. These values are loosely modeled after the Josephson Institute of Ethics' six pillars of character. They propose that these pillars "act as a multi-level filter through which we process decisions. So, being trustworthy is not enough — we must also be caring. Adhering to the letter of the law is not enough — we must accept responsibility for our action or inaction."

According to the Josephson Institute, "the word 'integrity,' derived from the word 'integer,' means 'one' or 'whole.' This means there are no divisions in an ethical person's life, no difference in the way she makes decisions from situation to situation, no difference in the way she acts at work and at home, in public and alone." For people with integrity, who they are and how they present themselves are one and the same.

LIVING THE CORE VALUES

As a way of bringing values to life, think about a public figure who, in your opinion, demonstrates a high levels of integrity. This might be someone whose work is visible in the media such as a politician, a businessperson, a film character, etc. Now think about someone in your everyday life who also displays high levels of integrity. In your learning journal, identify three specific things that each of these individuals do that gives you this impression.

Most people are able to spot a person of very low or high integrity. *Pat*, for example, is a person of low integrity. Pat (not his real name), a public relations manager, enjoys working with people and is skilled in interpersonal interactions. He seems to be able to smooth things over and say exactly the right thing at the right time. But that is part of Pat's problem: he says only what people want to hear rather than being honest with them. He takes on assignments such as chairing committees or hosting visitors to the organization but his employees are often the ones who do the work.

LIVING THE CORE VALUES

He's usually at least 10 minutes late for meetings, work, lunch appointments, and any other scheduled events. He can't be counted on to keep his word. He's willing to say one thing to his employees and another to his boss if "that's what it takes to get ahead." He often backs out of commitments such as giving an employee feedback on her design of the website or attending his daughter's soccer game. When entertaining guests (corporate or otherwise) on his expense account, he hosts extravagant dinners at his friend's restaurant, leaving a tip that is about the same amount as the meal. He believes in the need to "roll with the punches," and he looks poorly upon individuals who might consider him to be unreliable, untrustworthy, or unethical. Because he is so friendly and easygoing, few people around him seem to notice these lapses in integrity.

Sherron Watkins, the former Vice President of Corporate Development at Enron, would probably have little patience for Pat. Sometimes considered to be abrasive by her coworkers, Sherron was particularly conscientious about the need for integrity. When she realized the potential impropriety and illegality of her colleagues' complex accounting schemes that inflated Enron's stock price and reduced their tax load, she decided to let her boss know about her misgivings.

Here's what *Time Magazine* had to say about her: "It took Watkins weeks to work up the nerve to write her first letter to Lay, her boss. She had been working for chief financial officer Andrew Fastow last summer, looking for assets to sell as Enron ran into financial trouble ... but everywhere she looked she ran into off-the-books arrangements that no one could explain or seemed to want to investigate. The letter laid out what many executives knew but no one had the courage to say. 'It sure looks to the layman on the street that we are hiding losses in a related company and will compensate that company with Enron stock in the future.' ... Watkins went to Lay seeking a meeting. The

9

session was businesslike, and Lay seemed genuinely concerned ... By then, Lay was in the middle of a personal stock sell-off. As late as Sept. 26, Lay would try to reassure Enron employees that 'our financial liquidity has never been stronger.' And we all know what happened afterwards..."

1
......

REALITY CHECK: SELF COACHING QUESTIONS

Now, as a way of helping you examine your core values, we invite you to ask yourself a series of self-coaching questions. While thinking about your behavior in the past six months or so, find specific examples that support your answers. Also, consider whether or not "counter examples" may exist; in other words, times when you may not have behaved in a manner that is consistent with your responses. In answering these questions, think about how you generally are rather than temporary cracks in your "integrity foundation."

Your answers to these self-coaching questions will shine a light on how you see yourself. If you know yourself well, then your answers will be right on the mark. However, many people don't have accurate self-perceptions, either because they're not used to assessing themselves or because they feel uncomfortable with the whole idea of reflecting on their own behaviors. As a result, their answers may be *extreme*: either inflated or very low.

In all cases, but especially when answers are extreme (in any direction), seeking candid and honest feedback from others can be a valuable means of shedding more light on your actual competency levels. In other words, you can learn a lot more about yourself if you get feedback from others. You can do so by asking them to answer some of the self-coaching questions for you.

LIVING THE CORE VALUES

They may not tell you what you want to hear, but it may be exactly what you need to help you make progress on your journey toward becoming an awesome manager. As American writer Herbert Sebastian Aga said in his book *A Time for Greatness*, "the truth that makes men free is, for the most part, the truth which men prefer not to hear." Asking others for feedback takes lots of courage on everyone's part. Others don't necessarily have the same picture of you as you have of yourself, and people are sometimes reluctant to "tell it like it is." However, "feedback-lite" that is polite and tells you what you hope to hear won't help you grow as a person. Tell people that you need the straight goods (politely though!).

LIVING THE CORE VALUES

Am I fair?

→ Do I tend to make decisions in a consistent manner? Or, do I flip-flop and change my mind and direction?

→ Would others say that I treat them in an equitable manner?

→ Do others generally consider my decisions to be fair?

→ How often do I offer a reason or rationale for my decisions?

→ Do I avoid giving preferential treatment to some individuals over others?

→ Do I follow an impartial process for making decisions?

Am I reliable?

→ Would others say that they always know what to expect from me?

→ Do I follow through on 100% of my commitments? Do I always do what I agree to do?

→ Do I generally follow through on

promises even though I can find good reasons not to do so?

→ Do I avoid rationalizing or making excuses for not keeping my promises?

→ Do I take responsibility for my choices?

→ Am I careful to only make promises that I can reasonably keep?

Am I trustworthy?

→ How trustworthy am I?

→ Can others depend on me to keep my word?

→ How often have I refused to support decisions that I don't agree with, even in the face of adversity?

→ Who would be most likely to view me as a trustworthy person? Untrustworthy? Why?

→ Does my overall behavior indicate that I am a person of high integrity?

→ Do I respect and treat others with dignity?

Am I ethical?

→ How sensitive am I to the moral dimension of my decisions?

→ Do people trust me to do what is morally right? Do I trust myself in this respect?

→ How comfortable would I be if my decisions were printed in the newspaper? Presented on the news?

→ Do I treat others the way I want to be treated, the way that they want to be treated, or whatever is convenient for me at the time?

→ Would anyone observing my day-to-day life conclude that I am a highly ethical person?

→ Do I care about the well-being of others?

Am I honest and truthful?

→ Would people say that I am a "blank slate" (in other words, I make my intentions and motives known to others)? Or do I typically have a hidden agenda that I keep to myself?

→ Would others say that I'm honest, genuine, and up-front with them?

→ How often do I tell the truth as I know it? Or, do I tell people what they want to hear even if I don't agree with it?

→ Do I tend to be completely honest about my motives for doing things? Or, do I tend to lie or bend the truth to say what I think others want to hear?

→ Do I take a stand on an issue based on what I think is right? Or, do I wait and see what my boss or others think before doing so?

→ Do I play by the rules and avoid cheating, fraud, and theft?

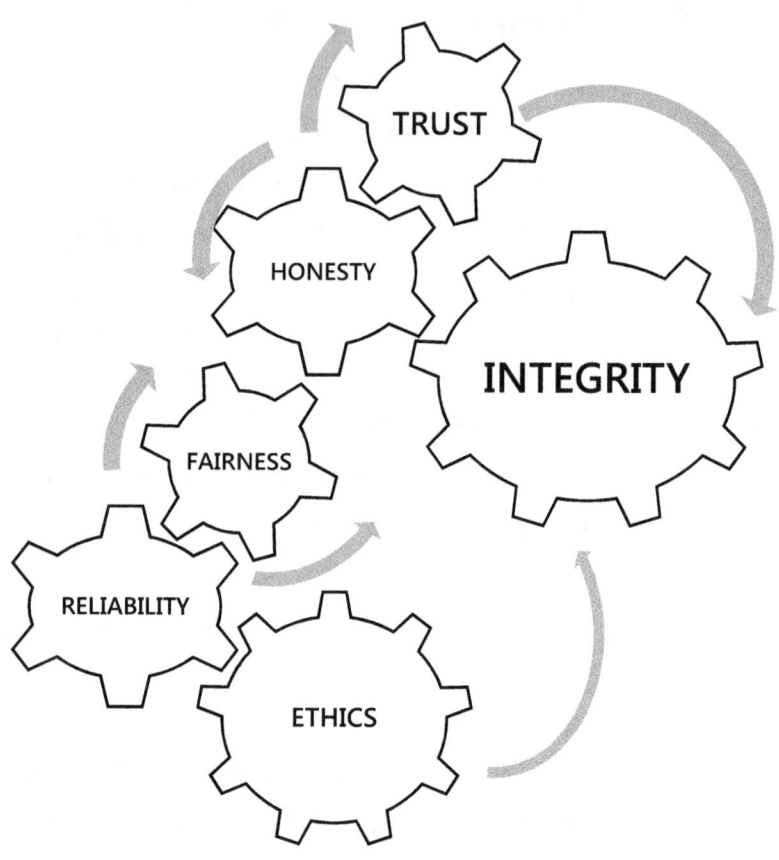

Reflection

What do your answers say about your perception of your strengths and your opportunities for improvement when it comes to integrity? Do you consider yourself to be a person of great integrity; in other words, someone who is always honest, truthful, trustworthy, reliable, fair, and ethical in your dealings with others? Or, do you believe that you have some opportunities to improve your overall level of integrity? What feedback did others give you about your level of integrity? How much overlap is there between your personal view and the opinions of others regarding your level of integrity? If they don't overlap well, why might this be the case?

Yes, these questions are challenging. In all likelihood, we can all think of times when we "weren't ourselves" and we behaved in a manner contrary to who we really are. This is especially likely in times of stress or crisis. Keep in mind, though, that too many cracks in your ethical pillars can damage and, indeed, destroy the foundation! The important point here is feeling motivated to make improvements, not punishing yourself for having less than perfect answers.

2

INSPIRING YOUR JOURNEY

As you read through the following quotations, take note of the ones that speak to you the most. Then consider the message they are conveying to you.

LIVING THE CORE VALUES

If you do not tell the truth about yourself
you cannot tell it about other people.
Virginia Woolf (British novelist)

⌘

What lies behind us and what lies before us are
tiny matters compared to what lies within us.
Oliver Wendell Holmes

⌘

If knowing yourself and being yourself were as
easy to do as to talk about, there wouldn't be
nearly so many people walking around in
borrowed postures, spouting secondhand
ideas, trying desperately to fit in rather than to
stand out.
Warren Bennis, On Becoming a Leader

⌘

This above all: to thine own self be true
And it must follow, as the night the day,
Thou canst not then be false to any man.
William Shakespeare, Hamlet

LIVING THE CORE VALUES

The commitments we make to ourselves and to others and our integrity to those commitments is the essence and clearest manifestation of our proactivity. It is also the essence of our growth. There are two ways to put ourselves in control of our lives immediately. We can make a promise – and keep it. Or, we can set a goal and work to achieve it. These give us the awareness of self-control and the courage and strength to accept more of the responsibility for our own lives.
Stephen Covey

⌘

Justice is truth in action.
Benjamin Disraeli

⌘

Be so true to thyself, as thou be not false to others.
Francis Bacon

It is necessary to the happiness of man that he be mentally faithful to himself. Infidelity does not consist in believing, or in disbelieving, it consists in professing to believe what one does not believe.
Thomas Paine

⌘

It is impossible that a man who is false to his friends and neighbors should be true to the public.
Bishop Berkeley

⌘

In keeping silent about evil, in burying it so deep within us that no sign of it appears on the surface, we are implanting it, and it will rise up a thousand fold in the future. When we neither punish nor reproach evildoers ... we are ripping the foundations of justice from beneath new generations.
Alexander Solzhenitsyn

LIVING THE CORE VALUES

As beings with a moral dimension we feel a threefold "tug" towards full humanity, a tug calling us: (1) to become 'good' persons, (2) to do the 'right' thing and (3) to build 'just' communities.

Russell Connors & Patrick McCormick

⌘

Integrity is an issue of whether it is possible for us to tell the truth about what we see happening, to make only those promises that we can deliver on, to admit to our mistakes, and to have the feeling that the authentic act is always the best for the business.

Peter Block

⌘

Before you tell the 'truth' to the patient, be sure you know the 'truth,' and that the patient wants to hear it.

Richard Clarke Cabot

⌘

The unexamined life is not worth living.

Socrates

LIVING THE CORE VALUES

The greatest predictor of how we will behave in the crucial moments of our lives is to be found in how we behave every day, because these are the things that shape character ... If we want to be able to make the correct or virtuous choice in a hard situation we will need to develop the habit of doing the right thing in smaller affairs.
Russell Connors & Patrick McCormick

⌘

Be more concerned with your character than your reputation, because your character is what you really are, while your reputation is merely what others think you are.
John Wooden

⌘

Justice should not only be done, but should manifestly and undoubtedly be seen to be done.
Gordon Hewart

LIVING THE CORE VALUES

Ethics is ultimately about our responsibilities toward other people. If you existed alone in the universe, there would be no need for ethics and your heart could be a cold, hard stone without consequence to anyone or anything. People who consider themselves ethical and yet lack a caring attitude toward individuals tend to treat others as instruments of their will.
Josephson Institute of Ethics

⌘

Oh what a tangled web we weave,
When first we practice to deceive!
Sir Walter Scott

⌘

Anytime you break a moral principle, you create a small crack in the foundation of your integrity.
John Maxwell

LIVING THE CORE VALUES

Integrity is doing the right thing, even when no
one is watching.
C.S. Lewis

⌘

If we use human influence strategies and
tactics to get other people to do what we want,
we may succeed in the short-term; but over
time our duplicity and insincerity will breed
distrust. Everything we do will be perceived as
manipulative. We may have the 'right' rhetoric,
style, and even intention, but without trust we
won't achieve primary greatness or lasting
success.
Stephen Covey

⌘

Do what is right, not what is easy nor what is
popular.
Roy T. Bennett, The Light in the Heart

⌘

Happiness is when what you think, what you
say, and what you do are in harmony.
Gandhi

LIVING THE CORE VALUES

Whether you are dishonest concerning a small issue is no different than if you are dishonest when dealing with a large issue ... With each act of dishonesty, a small crack pierces the eggshell ... Remember, once you get a crack in your eggshell, it is impossible to repair it.
Michael Camp, The Leader in the Mirror

⌘

What are your five favorite quotations?

Why do these stand out for you?

Which would you want to adopt as your personal motto? Include on the signature line of your emails? Post on your desk?

3

TIPS FOR AWESOME MANAGERS

As you review the following tips for living the core values and boosting your integrity, circle, check or highlight those that are especially meaningful for you.

LIVING THE CORE VALUES

1. **Be *whole*.** Keep in mind that the word *integrity* comes from the Latin word *integer*, which means to be whole. You act with integrity when you do what you say you will do. Own who you are and what you think, and let this show in your actions. Practice what you preach; behave in the manner in which you expect others to behave. Don't flatter or smooth talk others as a way of building up your social credits for use at a later time. WYSIWYG describes people of integrity; that is, what you see is what you get.

2. **Don't manipulate others.** Avoid gaining the confidence of others only to draw out personal information and use it against them later on. They will remember that you manipulated them, and they may seek out payback.

3. **Don't take advantage.** Support good causes for their benefit to society – not for how they benefit you. Don't use good causes for your own purposes and advantage.

4. **Choose honesty**; it's the foundation for people of integrity. People who are honest make a good-faith effort to communicate what they believe to be true without misleading or deceiving others. They are sincere, candid, and frank with others. They don't take statements out of context, communicate half-truths, or remain silent when that silence leaves impressions that are misleading. They share information that others need to know. They make difficult decisions rather than avoiding them or passing them on to someone else. They avoid stealing, cheating, defrauding, and other forms of dishonesty. They also do not look the other way or engage in

rationalization when they see others acting dishonestly. An incongruence between your actions and what you say undermines credibility.

5. **Don't deceive.** Sometimes, deception is justified; for example, when police officers are engaged in a sting operation or when you need to lie to escape a dangerous situation or to save your own or others' lives. However, the occasions where lying and deception are ethically acceptable are rare and tend to be limited to life and death situations. Deceiving others as a way of selling more products, obtaining a higher budget allocation, or winning at a game is dishonest.

6. **Be truthful.** Don't misrepresent the facts of a situation intentionally. What's especially important here is your intention. You should make a good-faith

attempt to: (a) gather all the facts of a situation; and (b) communicate your observations as representing your own point of view rather than the absolute truth. An example of a lack of truthfulness is inflating someone's performance rating as a way of getting them promoted out of your work unit or deflating a performance rating because you happen to dislike that person.

7. **Be courageous.** A precondition of truthfulness is courage, which is "the act of choosing to do the right thing when doing the right thing is not easy or convenient, comfortable, or safe," according to leadership researchers Carole Napolitano and Lida Henderson. For his part, Peter Block says that courage is, "to confront an issue when others are acting as if there is no issue; to say that a meeting is not going well when everyone else seems totally

satisfied." However, remember to use your judgment when deciding whether to express your opinion. There's a difference between being candid regarding important matters and difficult decisions and spouting forth all your likes and dislikes on every matter.

8. **Use caution (instead of courage) when**:
→ You have been in your job and/or organization for fewer than six months.
→ The organization is in a crisis mode and you need to "lay low."
→ You have already made some big changes.
→ You don't feel trusted or supported by your manager.

9. **Avoid the four enemies of integrity.** According to the Josephson Institute of Ethics, these include:

LIVING THE CORE VALUES

→ Self-interest (acting in a way that focuses on our own interests and desires at the expense of those of others)
→ Self-protection (doing whatever it takes to avoid undesirable outcomes)
→ Self-deception (refusing to see a situation for what it is)
→ Self-righteousness (always thinking that we're right and others are wrong; using an ends-justifies-the-means approach to decision making)

10. **Be trustworthy.** Don't let day-to-day events and situations affect your judgments of what is right and wrong. Don't have hidden agendas or attempt to manipulate others. According to Napolitano and Henderson, "People who are trustworthy inspire trustworthiness in others. Formal contracts or written agreements aren't needed to get them to do what they say they're going to do since they always follow through on their

word to the best of their ability. Trust grows out a kind of constancy in others that gives us confidence that they mean what they say; that they will act in accordance with their words, stand behind their commitments, and keep their promises despite whatever winds of political expediency swirl about them; that their words and actions can be counted on over time to display coherence and predictability."

11. **Earn the trust of others.** Individuals who tend to change their opinions to suit whatever is politically convenient at the moment have trouble earning the trust of others. These fence sitters will say whatever they think others want to hear. Block says that although these people are usually easy to get along with and may even demonstrate "interpersonal excellence," they are generally unwilling

to take a stand and, as a result, no one knows what they stand for.

12. **Trust others.** The other side of the trustworthiness coin is trusting others. It's important to form relationships with an attitude of trust rather than suspicion. According to leadership expert Lawrence Lovasik, "Suspicion is like an overzealous watchman who not only frightens off thieves, but likewise robs his master of all rest."

13. **Avoid violating others' trust in you.** According to trust researchers Roderick Kramer and Tom Tyler, several actions violate trust:

→ Violating rules, changing them after they have been agreed upon, or breaking a contract.

→ Violating the "social contract," agreed-upon rules about how to function in a society. This "honor violation" may include shirking responsibilities, breaking promises, lying, stealing ideas, taking the credit for someone else's work, or disclosing confidences and secrets.

→ Being abusive toward others.

→ Damaging someone's identity by publicly criticizing them, accusing them unfairly, or insulting them or the organizations to which they belong.

14. **Admit your errors.** It's hard to repair trust that has been broken. According to Kramer and Tyler, the first step is acknowledging that you have violated someone's trust. Next, you need to examine the causes of the violation including your contribution to it. Then, you should admit your error and accept responsibility for its effects.

15. **Be reliable.** Ensure that you can be counted on to keep your promises, and only make promises or commitments

that you can keep. When you do make commitments, be very clear about the nature of this commitment so that others know what to expect. This also means that you must make a reasonable effort to follow through on your commitments. For example, if you agree to meet a coworker at the cafeteria at noon, then, barring unforeseen events, you actually meet them there at that time. You don't arrive at 12:10 pm. According to Lovasik, "You [must] try to be fair and reasonable rather than making excuses in bad-faith or justifying your way out of agreements that you have made. You show discourtesy and weakness of character if you frequently make excuses to others; if you're easily diverted from your obligations to others by chance meetings or conversations or passing interests; if you consider punctuality of little importance; or if you're in the habit of putting off preparations to keep

appointments   until   it   becomes
impossible to be on time."

16. **Ensure that the results of your decisions
are fair.** Be consistent, reasonable, and
equitable in making decisions. Ensure
that the outcomes of decisions, (for
example,   pay   increases,   layoffs,
promotions, etc.) are fair and exemplify
distributive   justice.   To   decide   if
outcomes   are   fair,   people   usually
compare what they have received to
some standard. This could be what
another person received, like a coworker
in the same or another organization, or
their own personal experiences on other
occasions. For example, a job candidate
who is offered a salary and told that it's
beyond what others are paid would feel
resentment when they discover that
others are actually paid much more.

17. **Make decisions in a fair manner.** It's not enough to make a decision that has a fair outcome; the process used to arrive at that decision must also be fair. The means to the ends should exemplify *procedural justice*. Indeed, even when the outcome is unpleasant, such as a layoff, if the approach used to make this decision is fair, then employees will demonstrate more positive attitudes toward the decision. To be considered fair, procedures must have *all* of the following characteristics:

→ Consistency (applying standards in a uniform manner)

→ Bias free (minimizing personal self-interest)

→ Accuracy (based on actual data or credible information sources)

→ Correctable in case of errors (allowing for a review of decisions)

→ Consideration of all parties (taking into account various interests)

→ Ethicality (taking into account general standards of moral conduct)
Managers can use these characteristics as standards or baselines for conducting performance reviews, allocating work assignments and rewards, and making other workplace decisions.

18. **Treat people fairly when you're in the process of making and communicating a decision.** Consider involving employees in decisions that concern them and ensuring that their involvement has an impact (this is *interactional justice*). Avoid bias or favoritism toward certain people over others. Remember that fair treatment is interpersonally sensitive, respectful, and polite. Offer feedback in a timely manner. Explain unfavorable outcomes. Don't take advantage of people who are in a situation that makes them weak and powerless. Remember that employees are more likely to

respond negatively to injustice if: (a) the injustice is ongoing rather than a single event; (b) they are treated in an insensitive manner; (c) they aren't given adequate justifications and explanations; and (d) they aren't given an opportunity to express their opinions.

19. **Manage perceptions of justice.** These perceptions are a central source of motivation and, possibly, demotivation for employees. Employees who perceive a lack of fairness have poorer morale, are more likely to leave their jobs, tend to generate conflict, and may even retaliate as a way of "evening the score." In contrast, those who perceive that they and others have been treated fairly are more likely to: extend a helping hand to others; speak well of the organization and its managers; behave in an ethical manner; express their commitment to the organization; and trust, respect, and

44

go out of their way to help managers who are fair - regardless of the outcome of a decision. Even people who benefit from favoritism feel less respect for managers who are unfair.

20. **Manage perceptions of justice (part 2).** Consciously consider whether your actions and decisions are fair and will be perceived as fair by others. You might make decisions that are entirely fair, but your employees may consider them to be unfair. For example, imagine that, one morning, you and an employee agree that the employee will perform Task A and meet clearly specified standards of quality, quantity, and timeliness. At the end of the shift, the employee has not met the standards, and you give the employee feedback accordingly. The employee, however, may consider their performance to be exemplary given the circumstances and get their coworkers to

send letters to this effect. Although you openly and sympathetically listen to your employee's perspectives, your opinion of the employee's performance doesn't change. Perhaps because the employee hadn't received such a rating from previous supervisors, is lacking self-knowledge, or is acting out of self-interest, the employee continues to insist that the feedback was unfair. According to justice researchers Robert Folger and Russell Cropanzano, "self-interest often biases fairness perceptions, preferences, choices, and reactions. What is missing is the vantage point of the neutral, *disinterested* spectator: the third party observer whose own material well-being and self-regard are not directly jeopardized, but who nonetheless cares about what happens." Two lessons in this story are that: (a) regardless of the actual fairness of a decision, it may be perceived as unfair; and (b) people need to recognize how their self-interest and self-protection may cause them to mistakenly label a decision as unfair. They should be open to the possibility that the decision is indeed fair when viewed from a different perspective.

21. **Be consistent in your treatment of others and your decisions.** Managers who are consistent are predictable. Others know exactly what to expect from them and what is expected in return. Their decisions are based on well-defined and explicit criteria. They treat all employees in a similar manner, and they respond to workplace issues in a manner that is easily anticipated by others. They offer no surprises to others. They don't "test the wind" to see what public opinion is before they offer their opinions.

22. **Be ethical.** According to the Josephson Institute, "ethics are standards of

conduct that indicate how one should behave based on moral duties and virtues, which themselves are derived from principles of right and wrong." It's important to establish the moral tone in your work team and organization by setting a good example through: (a) your everyday behaviors, (b) how you deal with crises, (c) who you hire, and (d) how you reward and/or punish ethical and/or unethical behavior. Keep in mind that managers' ethics are very important in organizational performance and in shaping an organization's moral tone. Be aware of factors that might affect ethical decision making such as: pressure for profit or cost savings, competition, political corruption, media coverage, governmental regulations, and personal greed. Prepare staff for ethical decision making by discussing ethical issues and providing ongoing employee education.

23. **Avoid explaining away or dismissing unethical behavior.** Often doing so involves some form of rationalization. Which of the following rationalizations do you recognize in yourself and others?

→ "If it's necessary, it's ethical." In other words, the ends justify the means.

→ "If it's legal and permissible, it's proper." Remember that society's laws establish only the *minimum* standards of behavior and, as such, are not an appropriate substitute for moral judgment.

→ "I was lying to protect you." This common rationalization for telling "little white lies" or withholding significant information in relationships suggests that people need to be shielded from the truth. This means, however, that people aren't making decisions based on accurate information. Imagine asking your employees for feedback on your organizational skills and being told that you're outstanding in this area even

49

though this is untrue. If you don't have accurate self-knowledge, then you may simply believe what you have been told. Besides giving you a false sense of security about these skills, it doesn't give you the chance to improve them. If, one day, you discover that your organizational skills truly do need improvement, then rather than appreciating your employees' sense of consideration, you are more likely to feel patronized or even betrayed.

→ "I'm just fighting fire with fire." In other words, if others stoop to engage in deception, betray confidences, and play games, then you feel justified in doing so as well. This approach prolongs a cycle of mistrust.

→ "It's okay if doesn't hurt anyone." In other words, if no one *seems* to be hurt as a result of your actions, then violating ethical principles is okay. This justification treats ethical obligations as optional rather than necessary.

→ "Everyone's doing it." This argument suggests that the mere fact that others are engaging in a particular behavior is a sufficient indication of its ethicality. This "safety in numbers" approach means that you're delegating your decision-making responsibility to others.

→ "It's OK if I don't personally gain from it." This argument justifies behavior by saying that, if others or the organization benefit from the decision rather than you, it's ethical.

→ "I've got it coming." If people feel that they've been mistreated in some fashion (for example, underpaid, target of unfair decisions or treatment, overloaded with work), they may justify bad behavior in retaliation. For example, they may rationalize that they are just getting "their due" to "even the score" when they abuse sick time, inflate expense claims, make frequent personal phone calls, take extended coffee or lunch breaks, arrive late or leave early, spend hours on the internet for personal reasons while at work, and make personal use of office supplies.

→ "I can still be objective." Unfortunately, people often don't realize the subtle effects of friendship or the anticipation of future favors on their judgment. For example, you may accept an extravagant gift from a client without acknowledging that they expect a favor in return.

24. **Work to move to the next stage of moral development.** In his extensive research, psychologist Lawrence Kohlberg found that people justify their decisions and actions in six different ways:

→ People at Stage 1 want to avoid punishment at all costs, so they stick to and obey the rules. "How can I avoid punishment? I'll do *X* because it's the law, and the law's the law."

→ Stage 2 folks follow the rules only when it's in their own interest to do so. They equate moral or "right" actions with satisfying their own needs. "What's in it for me? I'll do *X* because I benefit from it."

→ The focus of those at Stage 3 is approval from others, being seen as a good person, and living up to the expectations of people who are close to them (such as family, friends, and co-workers). "What can I do to be seen as a good person? I'll do *X* because others expect me to do it."

→ At Stage 4, people try to fulfil duties and obligations including upholding laws. They have a law and order orientation. "What action will allow me to uphold the law for the benefit of society? I'll do *X* because it will help to maintain social order, and I would want others to do it."

→ Self-interest is the primary motivator for people at stages 1 and 2, whereas conformity is a motivating force for those at Stages 3 and 4.

→ Finally, at stages 5 and 6, principles guide people's behavior. Those at Stage 5 uphold rules because they are part of the social contract. They also uphold values regardless of majority opinion. "What can I do that will do the greatest good for the greatest number of people? I'll do X because it benefits lots of people."

→ Stage 6 individuals try to follow universal ethical principles that cover all contingencies, are never violated, and don't change with the situation. "What can I do that is right and just? I'll do X because it is the right thing to do."

→ Kohlberg says that most people tend to function at levels 3 and 4. However, more ethical decisions are made by people who are at higher levels of moral development. To move to higher levels, people need to confront and discuss value-based issues.

25. **Understand that ethics is not simply a "personal matter."** As suggested by the Josephson Institute, "The personal view of ethics suggests that, if a person believes that a particular action is ethical but another disagrees, then neither is necessarily right or wrong. In other words, ethics is situational and personal. However, some people adopt personal codes of conduct that are inconsistent with universal ethical norms. Clearly, not all choices and value systems are equally 'ethical.' If they were, we would have no way to distinguish between the ethical levels of Hitler and Gandhi. A person who believes that certain races are inferior to others and therefore that it is 'right' to oppress or persecute those races has adopted a personal value system that is inherently 'unethical.' ... Simply put, all individuals are morally autonomous

beings with the power and right to choose their values, but it does not follow that all choices and all value systems have an equal claim to be called ethical."

26. **Stand up for what you believe in without discounting others.** When asked for your opinion, answer honestly. Say what you mean. For example, don't say that an idea is "interesting" when you don't actually believe this. "Interesting" can be a code word that is used to appear supportive, but it may simply express indifference or objection in an indirect manner. Instead, offer a balanced perspective of the advantages and disadvantages or risks of ideas.

27. **Express and be open to all sides of a story.** Look for relevant information and alternative perspectives before making

important decisions. Be willing to say "I don't know."

28. **Use language that describes reality.** Avoid using euphemisms or words that mask the real intention of your actions. For example, when laying off people, instead of talking about rightsizing or delayering, call it what it is. Don't say "I don't mean to interrupt you, but..." or "Don't take this personally but..." when your true intention is to interrupt or offer a personal comment. Only say "thank you for the feedback" if you are truly grateful for it. Only say "people are our most important asset" if your actions reflect this statement.

29. **When you make a mistake, admit it and make things right.**

30. **Say no when you mean no.** Do not hedge your position out of fear of

disapproval. If you don't feel comfortable saying no, then your yes means very little.

31. **Honor your commitments and promises.** Avoid rationalizations or excuses. Walk the talk; ensure that there is no gap between what you say and what you actually do. Keep any commitments that you make to yourself. This will help you develop the confidence you need for keeping your commitments to others.

32. **Pay attention to how vulnerable you are to external influences**. Don't allow yourself to be influenced by others to make decisions that you wouldn't support as an individual.

33. **Avoid manipulating others**, that is, trying to influence others without their knowledge. Use techniques such as making eye contact, leaning forward,

showing interest, and restating other people's positions for listening, not for manipulating others. Don't drop names for the purposes of communicating the implied or expressed support of important people. This is an indirect way of trying to control people.

34. **Don't try to obtain advantages for yourself that you don't deserve and that would be unfair to others** (for example, additional salary, perks, resources, etc.). Don't pad your expense statement or your demands for extra funding, staff, or physical space.

35. **Give credit where it's due.** Share credit for team successes; don't take credit for other people's work.

36. **Don't engage in offensive behavior or share offensive jokes.** Discourage these in others.

37. **Don't create surprises for others; be predictable.**

38. **Be concerned with the spirit of the law as well as the letter of the law.** For example, some individuals game or manipulate the system while following rules, but, in doing so, they ignore the intended purpose of the rules.

39. **Have enough controls in place in order to prevent unethical behavior.** Hire people who are ethical. Be explicit about how you define ethical behavior to employees. Help your employees understand how to go about making ethical decisions. Be open to hearing what employees have to say. Encourage your employees to talk about ethical issues. Provide the rationale behind your decisions. Reward ethical behavior and punish unethical behavior.

40. **Follow a systematic process for making ethical decisions.** Clarify exactly what needs to be decided. Identify a wide range of alternatives including ethically justifiable ones. Automatically eliminate those that are impractical or illegal. Evaluate the remaining alternatives in terms of whether or not they require sacrificing ethical principles. Base your evaluation on solid facts rather than rationalizations, beliefs, biases, or fears. Examine the benefits, burdens, and worst-case scenarios of each alternative for all parties. Decide on an alternative course of action using at least some of the "ethics guides" presented in the table on the next pages. Develop an implementation plan that maximizes benefits and minimizes costs and risks. Monitor the effects of your decision and modify your actions as needed.

LIVING THE CORE VALUES

Ethics Guides

GOLDEN RULE — Are you treating others as you would want to be treated yourself?

PUBLICITY — Would you be comfortable if your reasoning and decision were to be publicized on the front page of a national newspaper?

KID-ON-YOUR-SHOULDER — Would you be comfortable if your children or parents were observing you? Are you practicing what you preach?

DIGNITY AND LIBERTY TEST: Does this decision preserve the dignity and liberty of others?

EQUAL TREATMENT TEST: Are you giving the rights, welfare, and betterment of minorities and lower status people full consideration?

PERSONAL GAIN TEST: What decision would you make if the outcome didn't benefit you in any way?

CONGRUENCE TEST: Is this decision or action consistent with your espoused personal principles? Does it violate the spirit of any organizational policies or laws?

PROCEDURAL JUSTICE TEST: Would those affected by a decision consider the procedures used to arrive at the decision to be fair?

COST-BENEFIT TEST: Does a benefit for some cause unacceptable harm to others? How critical is the benefit? Can you lessen the harmful effects?

STAKEHOLDER TEST: What are the potential consequences of your decision for the people, groups, and organizations that are likely to be affected by your decision?

GOOD NIGHT'S SLEEP TEST: Whether or not anyone else knows about your action, will it produce a good night's sleep?

41. **Support your employees when needed.** During times of layoffs, pay special attention to the needs of those who are laid off and the survivors who remain in the organization.

42. **Don't label others as being unfair just because they won't give you what you feel you deserve.** Fairness is a potent label, but it doesn't apply to every

decision that you happen to disagree with.

43. **Share as much information as possible** not just the minimum amount of information that people need to know to do their jobs. Don't buffer employees from bad news. According to Peter Block, "When we shield our people we are acting as their parents and treating them like children. Delaying bad news reduces people's trust in us and their belief that we have trust and confidence in them. Through these small acts of caution, we end up creating the kind of bureaucratic and 'political' organization that we wish to change."

44. **Keep employees informed of any changes in plans, policies and procedures** that may affect them.

45. **Ensure that your policies, procedures, and expectations are fair.** Don't ignore behavior in some employees and punish it in others. Be consistent in how you make decisions. Ensure that the severity of employee discipline is commensurate with the severity of the offense. Ensure that you distribute your support, feedback, and resources, both economic and emotional, evenly among your employees.

46. **When mediating a conflict between two people, give each person equal time** to present their case. Try to be impartial and neutral.

After reading these tips, review the ones that you have circled, checked, or highlighted. What do they have in common?

4

DILEMMAS: WHAT WOULD YOU DO?

Now you have the opportunity to consider how to apply what you just learned in a sampling of situations. For each dilemma, read the situation, select the best alternative (or create your own), and explain why you consider this option to be the most appropriate solution.

LIVING THE CORE VALUES

Situation 1: You're responsible for the facility operations of a large processing plant. In your last budget submission, you requested funds for the installation of a new air compressor and two years' worth of parts. Although you expect your budget to be approved, final approval has yet to be given. Since you're anxious for the new air compressor to be installed, you have begun negotiations with a supplier. You tell the supplier:

    a. I don't have approval for this project yet, but I'm expecting it any day now. You'll be making quite a bit of profit off this deal, so let's get started with the installation without an official contract.

    b. It's been approved. I'd like the equipment installed as soon as possible.

    c. Install the equipment now and, when my budget's approved, we'll work up a contract.

    d. I fully expect my budget to be approved, so let's get started with a tentative estimate of the likely costs and schedule.

Situation 2: It's mid-September, and you notice that office supplies have gone missing from the storage cabinet. Although it's possible that the supplies disappeared at beginning of the school year by coincidence, an employee just informed you that employees Chris and Pat have been using the supply cabinet as a cheap way of "shopping" for school supplies for their children. You decide to:

   a. Institute a new policy that requires that the supply cabinet be locked and that supplies be signed out by employees.
   b. Tell Chris and Pat that they have no business stealing from the organization and that further instances of theft will be reported to the police.
   c. Install a video camera in the area of the supply cabinet so that you can catch the thieves in the act.
   d. Send a general reminder to employees that office supplies are for office use only, and that any problems will result in disciplinary action.

LIVING THE CORE VALUES

Situation 3: You're in charge of accounting at a medium-sized manufacturing company. You have an opening for a full-time, entry-level accounts payable clerk. Your friend would like you to consider her daughter for the position. You already have an application from someone that you don't know. You decide to:

    a. Hire your friend's daughter, out of loyalty to your friend.

    b. Hire the other applicant because you don't want to appear to be biased in favor of your friend's daughter.

    c. Ask your Staffing Officer to help you choose between the two candidates.

    d. Ask your Staffing Officer to conduct a full search for more candidates before you make a decision.

Situation 4: As the new Director of Nursing for your health center, you've been hearing about mix-ups in dispensing and distributing medications to patients and delays in receiving the needed mediations from the hospital pharmacy. You decide to:

a. Immediately purchase state-of-the-art medication carts that allow nurses to select a patient name and photo on the touch screen and automatically receive the appropriate mediations using a barcode and robot system.

b. Do nothing. The problem might work itself out.

c. Meet with the pharmacist to discuss how to ensure accurate and speedy service from their unit, and review existing procedures for distributing medications with nursing supervisors.

d. Send a memo to your nursing staff ordering them to comply with existing regulations or be subject to disciplinary action.

LIVING THE CORE VALUES

Situation 5: You have noticed that two of your employees are engaged in a romantic relationship. You have overheard other employees talking about these employees and their activities on and off the job, including having sex in a company vehicle. They both have spouses and children. You decide to:

    a.   Ignore the situation as long as it isn't affecting their work performance.

    b.   Contact their spouses and inform them of this adulterous behavior.

    c.   Meet with the two employees and order them to discontinue their relationship immediately "or else!"

    d.   Meet with the two employees and ask them to think about the implications of their behavior.

Additional ethical dilemmas:

For each of the following ethical questions (most of which have been developed by Jeff McLaughlin, professor at Thompson Rivers University), consider what is the morally right thing to do. Explain your reasons. Is what you would *actually* do different from what you *should* do? If so, why? Next, pick any one of the questions, and try to consider why someone might answer it differently than you. Can you offer reasons for their views? Are any of these reasons persuasive?

1. Should the wealthier members of society be forced to pay, through taxation, for the poorer members? If so, how much? Why?

2. You are on a country road and see two neighboring farm houses on fire. One is yours, and the other belongs to a new couple who just moved in. Your wife and child are at home, as are your neighbors. You can only save one house. Which one

do you save?

3. You run an orphanage and have had a hard time making ends meet. A car dealership offers you a new van worth $15,000 for free if you will falsely report to the government that the dealership donated a van worth $30,000. You really need the van, and it will give you an opportunity to make the children happy. Do you agree to take the van?

4. You are shopping, and you notice a person stuffing a pair of stockings into their purse. Do you report them?

5. You are waiting with a few other people to board a bus. The bus pulls up and, before you can board, the driver gets out and goes into the convenience store to get a coffee. You are the last to get on the bus. Do you pay your fare?

6. You discover Bill Gates' wallet lying on the street. It contains $1,000. Do you send it back to him?

7. It's 3 a.m., and you're late getting home. As you approach an intersection, you notice that no one is around. Do you drive through the red light?

8. As a nurse, you're the last person to see Mr. Doe before he dies in hospital. You believe that he has become mentally incompetent in the last few hours, and, in that time, he has rewritten his will. In the new will, he viciously attacks each member of his adopted family; he cuts every family member out of the will; and he leaves his fortune to a psychic chat line. Mr. Doe asks you to make sure that the new will gets to his lawyer. Knowing that the document will most likely be thrown out of court but not before the damage to Mr. Doe's family is done, do you carry out Mr. Doe's last request?

9. Would it be justifiable to whip pigs to death if more succulent pork resulted from this process, thus giving the consumers of pork more pleasure?

74

LIVING THE CORE VALUES

10. Should the theft of $1,000 be punished more than the theft of $100?

11. You can only rescue one of each of the following pairs. Which do you save?
a) A child or an adult
b) A stranger or your dog
c) Hitler or Lassie
d) Your spouse or a Nobel Laureate
e) A dog or a weasel
f) Your entire family or the entire canine species
g) A bottle with the cure for cancer or your brother
h) A bottle with the cure for cancer or your brother who just gave you one of his kidneys

12. Are the following acceptable grounds for a person to take the life of a non-human animal?
a) Its noise bothers you at night.
b) A wolf is killing your sheep.
c) Its meat makes a tasty dish.
d) You enjoy seeing it squirm.

e) Gophers are destroying your vegetable garden.

f) You just don't like snakes.

g) The condor (an endangered species) keeps killing your prized carrier pigeons.

h) You enjoy hunting.

i) You want your picture taken with "big game" to prove your virility.

j) You're moving, and your new apartment doesn't accept dogs.

k) You've been in a plane accident, and you need to take the life of your ____ in order to survive.

l) You think that there's an overpopulation of these animals.

m) You live near the North Pole, and you want to wear bear fur so that you can keep warm.

n) Your friends are pressuring you to throw a cat in a well – just for fun.

5

PLANNING FOR ACTION

Part A

1. What top five lessons have you learned about personal mastery while working through the book?

2. Starting now, what specific actions will you take to personally demonstrate and promote integrity in the workplace?

Part B

Think of a time when you faced an ethical dilemma – whether you were making an ethical decision, or you were deciding what to do about someone's behavior that you considered to be unethical.

1. Describe the situation (context, who was involved, who did what, what you did, etc.).
2. What rationale or reason did you give for what you did?
3. Looking back, how do you feel about your behavior?
4. What would you do differently if you could turn back the hands of time?

About the Managerial Competencies Series

What's in the series?

This series is built around four managerial competency clusters: personal, people, purpose, and process.

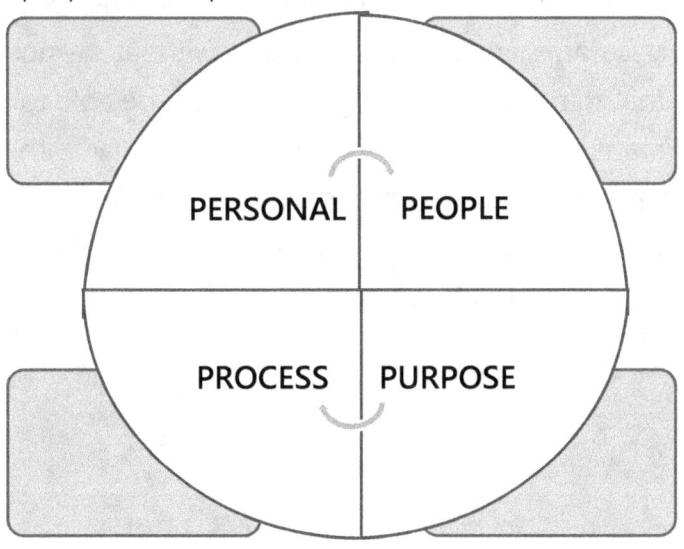

LIVING THE CORE VALUES

Each cluster is made up of several competencies possessed by awesome managers. The series addresses a total of 15 competencies, each of which is the topic of a book of around 100 pages. Let's look at each cluster one at a time.

Personal Competencies

The starting point of the series is developing personal skills, given that effective self-management is essential for managing people, programs, and processes. It goes without saying that to manage others, you first must be able to manage yourself. People who are familiar with their personal strengths and challenges and who engage in effective self-management tend to work well with others.

LIVING THE CORE VALUES

Here are the competencies included in the Personal Competencies cluster:

1. **Living the Core Values**, which involves demonstrating honesty, truthfulness, trustworthiness, reliability, fairness, and ethicality in all your decisions and interactions.
2. **Developing Personal Mastery** through personal responsibility, emotional resilience, constructive attitudes, self-confidence, adaptability, conscientiousness, and competence.
3. **Organizing Yourself** by focusing on your

priorities and making effective use of time.

4. **Building Stress Resilience**, which deals with managing life's stresses by developing personal hardiness.

People Competencies

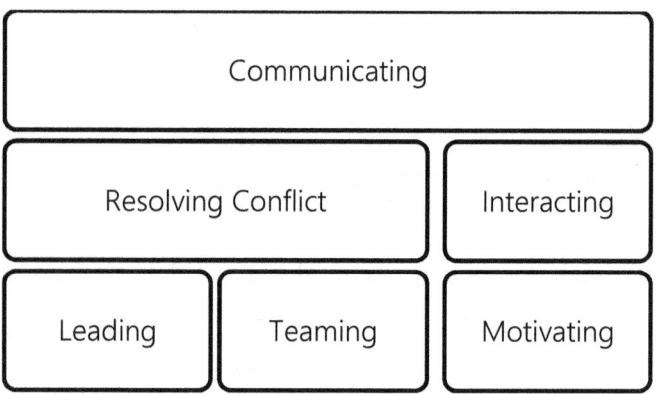

This cluster helps you examine and build your skills in working with and managing others. Although it's important for managers to be *technically* competent in order to gain credibility, interpersonal skills make the difference between awesome and not-so-awesome managers.

The competencies included in the People Competencies cluster are:

5. **Communicating in Writing and through Presentations**, which focuses on communicating ideas effectively, whether verbally or in writing.
6. **Creating Engagement**, creating motivating working conditions so that staff contribute their best to the organization.
7. **Building Relationships**, which considers how to interact with others through effective listening and responding.
8. **Resolving Conflict**, which addresses how to deal with conflict in a productive manner.
9. **Leading Your Team**, which means leading in a manner that is appropriate for the needs of the situation and your team.
10. **Cultivating Team Spirit** by building a cohesive, high-performing team.

Purpose and Process Competencies

This final cluster combines two sets of competencies. Purpose competencies offer you a "big picture" perspective of your organization and your own role in the organization. Process competencies help you translate this "big picture" (the *whats*) into everyday practice (the *hows*). In other words, they allow you to consider how work should be done as a means of accomplishing the goals of your organization and your work unit.

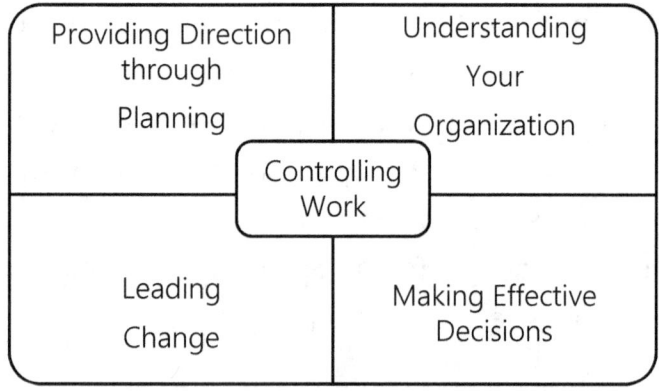

LIVING THE CORE VALUES

Purpose and Process competencies include:

11. **Making Effective Decisions**, whether individually or in a team setting.
12. **Controlling Work Performance** by establishing control mechanisms to ensure results.
13. **Providing Direction through Planning**, which discusses the management process and offers tips for setting organizational direction and developing operational plans that fit this direction.
14. **Understanding Your Organization**, in other words, understanding the principles of organizing work and creating the right structure for your work unit.
15. **Leading Change** so that your organization and team thrive.

How is each book organized?

Each book is organized according to a five-step learning process. This process is designed to help you learn in an active and reflective manner.

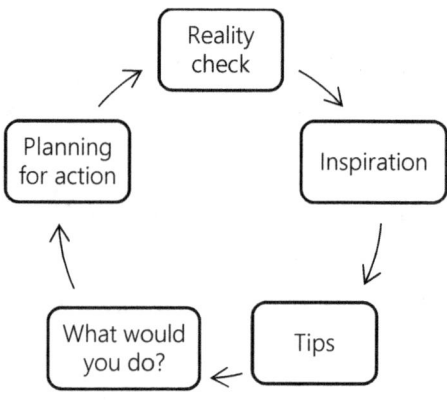

In each book, after a brief introduction, we jump right into the "**reality check**." This series of self-coaching questions is meant to help you reflect on and develop insight into your own strengths and weaknesses in relation to a particular competence and, hopefully, motivate you to work on building your competencies.

The reality check consists of the kinds of questions that management coaches might ask you, but that you can simply ask yourself. Just be sure to give yourself a chance to answer them!

Management coaches help managers view and understand situations from a variety of perspectives. But, if the art of coaching is asking challenging questions (as management coach Chantal Binet says), why not ask yourself these questions?

Second, to accompany you on your learning journey, you're offered a curated collection of **inspirational quotes**. There's lots of wisdom available from people from all walks of life. The quotes that grab us and speak to us do so because they have touched a nerve in us. They resonate with us, perhaps because they offer a message that we need to hear to continue developing or because they challenge us to become better people.

Third, we offer you tons of **tips and tricks** of awesome managers. These practical tips cover a gamut of perspectives and actions that you can take to improve your competencies. Ideally, they will encourage you to consider the variety of possibilities and alternatives that are available to you. It's up to you to decide which are the most useful to you. As you read this section, be sure to note or highlight the tips that stand out for you.

Next, we present a series of **dilemmas** or situations for you to resolve. This section will help you see how you might apply the tips and tricks from the previous section. We ask you to read the situation and then identify what you would do in these situations. You might choose one of the alternatives that is offered, or you might come up with your own creative solution. Ultimately, there are many factors and perspectives that might influence what is the "best" choice.

Finally, we nudge you to develop an **action plan** that you will *actually* implement.

LIVING THE CORE VALUES

Developing and implementing an action plan is an especially important step because it helps you draw value from your efforts in working through this series. After all, you're reading this book because you're hoping to become an awesome manager, right? This means developing a realistic plan that describes the actions that you intend to take to become an awesome manager, implementing your plan, reflecting on how well it worked, and then continuously making any adjustments that are needed. So, the cycle starts again!

How can you get the most out of the series?

You can read one or two books per month for an entire year, creating and implementing action plans for each book. Ultimately, this will help you develop a better understanding of yourself as a manager, your expectations, your strengths, and your areas for improvement.

As a way of refreshing your competencies, you can even re-read the books and re-visit your action plans in the future. Depending on what's happening in your life (new job, new team, new challenges), every time you read these books, you may develop new insights that help you deal with a situation.

LIVING THE CORE VALUES

The knowledge of the world is only to be
acquired in the world, and not in a closet.
Lord Chesterfield

What we have to learn to do,
we learn by doing.
Aristotle

Life is a succession of lessons which must be
lived to be understood.
Ralph Waldo Emerson

What do this British statesman from the 1600s,
Greek philosopher from 384 B.C., and American
poet from the 1800s have in common? They all
agree that learning comes from trying new
things, not from simply sitting back and reading
a book.

Don't just read the books; *do* them! Just
reading the books won't transform you into an
awesome manager. If you just read the books,
you might get to know a lot about what it means
to be an awesome manager without changing

what you do in the workplace. How useful is that? Just like learning to ride a bike, it's impossible to develop your skills by simply reading or even thinking about what you have read. Besides, as *The Matrix* reminds us, "There's a difference between knowing the path and walking it."

In order to truly learn from our experiences, we need to do a complete loop of the learning cycle: we need to reflect on our experiences, figure out what lessons we learned, consider ways to apply these lessons, and then apply them. You may know people who seem to repeat the same mistakes over and over again or people who continually approach situations in a manner that doesn't work for them. They're going through life without taking the time to reflect, consider what they've learned, and develop an action plan in order to change their experiences. They're stuck somewhere on the learning cycle. David Kolb, the creator of this learning cycle, says that we all have a favorite place on the cycle where we tend to get stuck.

LIVING THE CORE VALUES

Some people simply enjoy reading the books and reflecting on how they may relate to their lives, hopefully finding an opportunity to make use of their learning at some point in the future. However, without specific goals and action plans, they're not extracting as much value as they could from their investment of time and money.

Although this is partly due to differences in learning styles, it's also due to a reluctance to try something new and different. This may be caused by a fear of stepping out of one's comfort zone: what is familiar is comfortable. It may also be caused by a desire to accumulate a truckload of knowledge or have the perfect circumstances, such as the ideal boss or set of employees, before acting. Some of us think and think and continue to think without taking action. That used to be my personal downfall until I realized that knowing lots about a topic isn't the same as learning or making a difference in real life!

At the other extreme, some of us take action without first reflecting on our experiences and what we learned from them. Some people prefer to go ahead and try things out right away. They're more action-oriented than their reflective counterparts. These folks typically find it especially challenging to slow down, consciously reflect on what they're reading, and develop a well thought out action plan before acting. In the same way, if you just read the books and do nothing else, the learning process will get stuck right off the bat.

Reflecting and taking action is the best solution. It's not enough to *know* how to do something. Although it's helpful and important to take the time to reflect and develop insights, at some point, you need to *do* the work yourself. Otherwise, as management expert Peter Block has said, "Waiting becomes an excuse for not acting."

Here are **five other important things** to do to maximize your learning. First, **keep a learning journal**. Record your thoughts as you read the books, answer the self-coaching questions, and develop your action plans. It will help you clarify your thinking, see patterns in what you have been experiencing and writing, and serve as a record of commitments you have made to yourself through your action plans. You'll be able to look back at what you've written and be impressed with all that you've learned! You could use a notebook or create an electronic document. Some people even email journal entries to themselves as a way of recording the day and time of their entries.

Second, **pull together a feedback team** who can help you get the most from this series. Your feedback team could be a group of four or five people that you have confidence in, such as coworkers, your manager, friends, and family members. Don't be shy about asking people for their support in helping you become a better manager; they are more willing to help you than you might think! These discussions will offer you different perspectives and exponentially increase how much you learn from the series.

Besides, awesome managers surround themselves with people they trust who are willing to give them honest feedback that will help them grow as individuals.

In supporting you, others can play one or more of the following roles:

→ The Head: These people can help you analyze a question or problem objectively. They can sketch out options, compare data, or simply provide you with accurate information.

→ The Heart: These people can help you express your emotions and understand them better. They listen, cheer you up, don't make judgments, and give you a sense of security.

→ The Legs/Arms: These people help you do things. They go places with you; they make you get moving when you don't feel like it. These people energize you.

How can your manager help? Can your manager provide feedback, advice and tips, and time to complete the series? What will you do to get your manager's help? For example, could you meet with your manager once every two weeks to discuss your progress and talk about how to manage effectively?

How can your peers help? Can your peers provide feedback, tips about managing, or coaching when needed? What will you do to get their help? Could you schedule a coffee break with them once every two weeks to discuss what you're learning and to share tips? Can you work through the series together?

How can your employees help? Can your employees provide feedback regarding your strengths and opportunities for improvement or work with you to develop a plan for making your unit function more effectively? What will you do to get their help? Could you meet with them once every two weeks to discuss what you're learning and how your team can implement elements of your action plan?

How can your friends help? Could they provide feedback, tips about managing, and encouragement for you to try new things? What will you do to get their help? Could you organize a dinner with them once every two weeks to discuss what you're learning and how to implement your action plan?

Third, **develop and implement a SMARTER action plan.** You know you've really learned something when your behavior changes (for the better, of course).

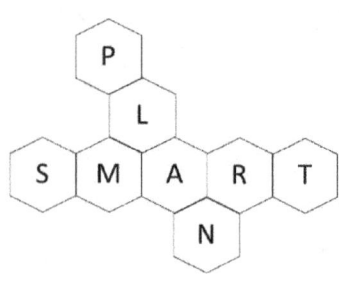

Insights and tips that are meaningful to you will change your perspective *and* your behaviors. That's why each book ends by inviting you to develop an action plan. Your plan should be **Specific, Measurable, Attainable, Realistic, Timely, Exciting, and Rewarded.** Think about things that you need to start doing, stop doing, or continue doing. Here's an example: "By the end of next week, I will write two letters – one to my former manager and one to my best friend – expressing my gratitude for their coaching and willingness to challenge me to become a better person. I will send these letters by email no later than Friday afternoon." Write your action plan in your journal. Revisit it to check your progress, and revise your plan as needed. Remember to ask for help from others, evaluate your progress, and reward yourself for your progress toward becoming an awesome manager.

Fourth, **identify obstacles or barriers that might get in your way of making the most of the series** and implementing your action plans; for example, lack of time or energy, poor personal habits, others' expectations, etc. List these in the column labelled "Obstacles" on the following page. Now, think about specific actions that you can take to address them and place these in the "Neutralizers" column; for example, meet with your manager, plan small wins or ways to celebrate your progress, etc.

LIVING THE CORE VALUES

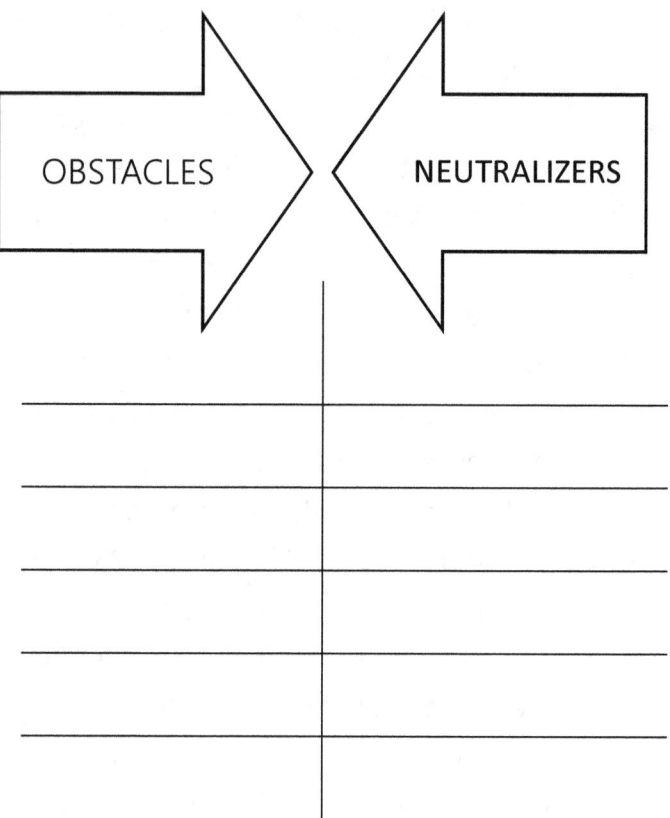

OBSTACLES | NEUTRALIZERS

Finally, do what you need to do to motivate yourself. Don't wait to be motivated to get started. Instead, get started, and motivation will come knocking at your door!

Also, try to be comfortable with discomfort. As you change how you manage, you may meet with some resistance from those around you. You exist in a system of relationships. Because systems are geared toward equilibrium (stability), if you change one thing in the system, the equilibrium is shot, and the system is upset. There may be pressure from others and from your own sense of comfort for you to do what you've always done regardless of whether or not it works.

It may be tempting to give up when things feel unnatural, but rest assured that this is part of the learning process. It's normal that trying out new ways of doing things makes you feel a bit uncomfortable in one way or another. Sometimes, we come across awesome folks who do their work without hesitation and seemingly without effort. It's easy to forget that they've gone through the highs and lows of the learning process. For example, think of Cirque du Soleil acrobats who seem to perform stunts with ease and pinpoint accuracy. It took them lots of practice, repetition, and even occasional failures to get to that skill level. Experts make things look easy.

Are you ready to begin your awesome journey? Earl Nightingale once said, "All you need is the plan, the road map, and the courage to press on to your destination." I hope that this series serves as your guide and road map on your journey toward awesomeness.

REFERENCES

Block, P. (2013). *Stewardship: Choosing Service over Self-Interest (2nd edition)*. San Francisco: Berrett-Koehler Publishers.

Duffy, M. (2002). By the Sign of the Crooked E. Time Magazine (Saturday, Jan. 19, 2002). Retrieved from: content.time.com/time/business/article/0,8599,195268,00.html

Folger, R., & Cropanzano, R., (1998). *Organizational Justice and Human Resource Management*. Sage.

Josephson Institute (2010). *Making Ethical Decisions*. The Six Pillars of Character. Retrieved from: https://classes.soe.ucsc.edu/cmpe080e/Spring10/Week%2007/6-pillars.html

Kohlberg, L. (1971). "From 'is' to 'ought': How to commit the naturalistic fallacy and get away with it in the study of moral development". In Theodore Mischel (Ed.). *Cognitive Development and Epistemology*. New York: Academic Press. pp. 151–284.

Kolb, D. A. (2014). *Experiential Learning: Experience as the Source of Learning and Development*. FT press.

Kramer, R. M., & Tyler, T. R. (Eds.). (1996). *Trust in Organizations: Frontiers of Theory and Research*. Sage.

Lovasik, L. G. (1999). *The Hidden Power of Kindness: A Practical Handbook for Souls who Dare to Transform the World, One Deed at a Time*. Sophia Institute Press.

Napolitano, C.S., & Henderson, L. J. (1997). *The Leadership Odyssey: A Self-Development Guide to New Skills for New Times*. Jossey-Bass.

LIVING THE CORE VALUES

Playbooks in the Managerial Competencies Series

1. Living the Core Values
2. Developing Personal Mastery
3. Organizing Yourself
4. Building Stress Resilience
5. Communicating in Writing and through Presentations
6. Creating Engagement
7. Building Relationships
8. Resolving Conflict
9. Leading Your Team
10. Cultivating Team Spirit
11. Making Effective Decisions
12. Controlling Work Performance
13. Providing Direction through Planning
14. Understanding Your Organization
15. Leading Change